A PRIMARY SOURCE
LIBRARY OF
AMERICAN CITIZENSHIP ™

Your Mayor: Local Government in Action

Jennifer Silate

rosen central
Primary Source ™

The Rosen Publishing Group, Inc., New York

Published in 2004 by The Rosen Publishing Group, Inc.
29 East 21st Street, New York, NY 10010

Copyright © 2004 by The Rosen Publishing Group, Inc.

6/2008 GEN FUND $30.00

First Edition

Library of Congress Cataloging-in-Publication Data

Silate, Jennifer.
Your mayor: local government in action/Jennifer Silate.—1st ed.
   p. cm.—(A primary source library of American citizenship)
Summary: Introduces the work of a mayor, how a mayor is elected, and what a city government does for its citizens and the nation. Includes bibliographical references and index.
ISBN 0-8239-4481-6 (library binding)
1. Mayors—United States—Juvenile literature. [1. Mayors. 2. Municipal government. 3. Cities and towns. 4. Occupations.]
I. Title. II. Series.
JS346.S55 2004
352.23'216'0973—dc22
                                                      2003013112

Manufactured in the United States of America

On the cover: Top right: New York City mayor Fiorello La Guardia photographed in 1943. Bottom left: New York City mayor Michael Bloomberg photographed at the city's annual Puerto Rican Day parade in 2002. Background: A 1797 letter by President George Washington to the Baltimore, Maryland, mayor and city council.

Photo credits: cover (background) © The Library of Congress Manuscript Division; cover (top right), p. 19 © Bettmann/Corbis; cover (bottom) © Getty Images © pp. 5 (top and bottom), 7 (top and bottom), 8, 9, 10, 11, 13, 14, 15, 17, 18, 20, 21, 22, 23, 25 (left and right), 27, 29, 30 © AP/Wide World Photos; p. 28 courtesy of the University of Michigan Library.

Designer: Tahara Hasan; Editor: Charles Hofer; Photo Researcher: Peter Tomlinson

Contents

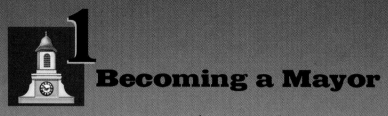

Becoming a Mayor

A mayor is in charge of running a city. He or she is the leader of a city's government. The city government runs many of the city's schools, hospitals, police and fire departments, and other public services. The mayor tries to help the citizens, or the people who live in the city. He or she works to make the people's lives better.

Every City Needs a Mayor

Some mayors are in charge of running a large city, such as New York City. Other mayors are in charge of running a small town or village.

Whether it's a small village or a large city, every town needs a mayor. Earl Jenkins, top, was mayor of Hermitage, Missouri, a town with a population of less than 500 people. Richard M. Daley, bottom, is the mayor of Chicago, a city with a population of nearly three million people.

The citizens choose who will be their mayor. This is called an election. In an election, the people can reelect a mayor. Or they can elect a new mayor. The number of years a person can be a mayor is called a term. Term lengths are different in many cities.

City Hall, Office of the Mayor

The mayor works in a building called city hall. The oldest city hall still in use is in Perth Amboy, New Jersey. It was built in 1767.

During an election, candidates for mayor go out and greet the voters. Above, Mayor Beverly O'Neill of Long Beach, California, hits the campaign trail in 2002. Below, candidate for mayor Sam Katz greets supporters at a rally in 2003.

Often, more than one person wants to be mayor. The people who want to be mayor are called candidates. Before an election, the candidates meet many of the people who live in the city. They listen to the needs of the people. The candidates ask the people of the city to vote for them.

Many times, candidates will meet in a debate, or public discussion. A debate will cover issues that concern the public. Mayor Sharon Sayles-Belton *(left)* of Minneapolis, Minnesota, debates with her challenger, Barbara Carlson, in 1997.

What's in a name? A lot, actually. Candidates will make signs, buttons, bumper stickers, and other things that say they are running for mayor. These raise awareness about the candidate. They also can tell how the candidate stands on certain issues.

Before an election, each candidate will give many speeches. The candidates tell the people what they will do for them if elected. Many people listen to the speeches. On election day, the people vote for whom they want to be mayor. When all of the votes are counted, the mayor is elected.

Voting is an important part of American politics. It gives every citizen the ability to choose his or her leaders. Even those running for mayor will vote. Here, Mayor Willie Brown of San Francisco casts his vote for mayor in 1999.

A lot of hard work goes into the race for mayor. Many people will help out during a mayoral campaign. David Cicilline, mayor-elect of Providence, Rhode Island, gives a speech in front of supporters after winning the election in 2002.

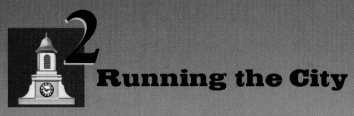

2 Running the City

After the mayor is elected, he or she has a lot of work to do. One important duty for the mayor is the city's budget. The budget decides what money will be used for what programs. The mayor must choose how much money to give to schools, hospitals, and other public services. Most of this money comes from taxes.

Different Cities, Different Budgets

A tax is money that must be paid by the people. This money is used for public services such as the police department, libraries, and public schools.

Budgets for 2003

Augusta, Georgia	$485,056,890
Kansas City, Missouri	$974,915,047
San Francisco, California	$4,937,228,512
New York, New York	$44,956,000,000

Cities with different populations have different budgets. New York City is the most populated city in America. More than 8 million people live in New York City!

The mayor will present the budget to the public. During the presentation he or she will explain what money will be used for what services. New York City mayor Michael Bloomberg speaks to the media about the city's budget for 2002.

Many mayors work with city councils. The city council is a group of people who help the mayor run the city. The mayor shows the city council members his or her budget. The council members can make changes to the budget. The mayor and the city council must agree on the budget before it is passed.

It takes more than a mayor to run an entire city. The city council helps the mayor run the city properly. Mayor Sharpe James *(left)* of Newark, New Jersey, listens to city council president Donald Bradley.

The mayor will act as the city representative. Here, Huntsville, Alabama, mayor Loretta Spencer *(second from right)* attends a ground-breaking ceremony in Greenbrier, Alabama. The ceremony was held to kick off construction of a new factory that will bring new jobs to the town.

Another important job the mayor has is passing laws for his or her city. Before a law is passed, it is called a bill. The city council will read the new bill first. If the council passes the bill, it then goes to the mayor. If the mayor agrees with the bill, he or she will sign it. Then the bill becomes law.

The Power of Veto

If a mayor votes against a bill, it will not become a law. This is called a veto. In city government, only the mayor has the power to veto.

A bill is a written idea for a new law. Bills are proposed to protect citizens and make the city a better place. Once the mayor signs the bill, it can become a law. Mayor Francis Slay of St. Louis, Missouri, signs the city's stadium bill. This bill is the first step toward raising money for the city's new baseball stadium.

3 Helping the City

The mayor has ideas to improve the city, such as to help the homeless or to fight crime. Sometimes, new laws are needed to do these things. The mayor can make his or her own laws to help the city. City councils must then agree to pass the laws made by the mayor.

A mayor will work closely with city services such as the police department. Mayor Paul Schell of Seattle, Washington, introduces Police Chief Gil Kerlikowske during a press conference. The two were meeting to announce a sharp drop in crime in the city.

The mayor can act as the figurehead in the fight against crime. In 1934, New York City mayor Fiorello H. La Guardia takes a swing at one of several slot machines confiscated by authorities. The setting was to demonstrate the city's crackdown on illegal gambling.

The city government helps people in several ways. There are many departments in the government that work for the people. There are departments to fix roads, help the poor, and pick up trash. The mayor has to make sure that every department runs well. The mayor chooses the people who will run these departments.

The mayor acts as a leader to organize many different parts of a city government. Here, Roswell, New Mexico, mayor Bill Owen *(center)* listens as New Mexico transportation secretary Pete Rahn speaks to the press.

Even the mayor has to lend a hand. Mayor Deedee Corradini of Salt Lake City, Utah, helps build a house with Habitat for Humanity in New Orleans, Louisiana.

The mayor spends a lot of time meeting with the citizens. He or she visits schools, religious groups, and other organizations. The mayor will learn about what the people need. He or she can also act as the city's representative. Sometimes the mayor gives special awards to people who have helped the city.

It's very important that a mayor stays in touch with the public—no matter what their age. Here, Baltimore, Maryland, mayor Martin O'Malley visits with students at an elementary school.

Representing the city is an important part of being mayor. Here, Mayor John Delaney of Jacksonville, Florida, gives a key to the city to Nobel Peace laureate Archbishop Desmond Tutu in 2003.

4 Different Cities, Different Mayors

Large cities and small cities share many problems. They both have crime, people without work, and homelessness. However, being a mayor in a small town or village is much different than in a large city. Problems in small cities affect fewer people. Sometimes, people in small cities even know their mayor's home phone number!

Where Does the Mayor Live?

Mayors in larger cities often live in houses paid for by the people in the city. In New York City, the mayor can live in Gracie Mansion. It was built in 1799. Ten rooms of the large house are open to the public.

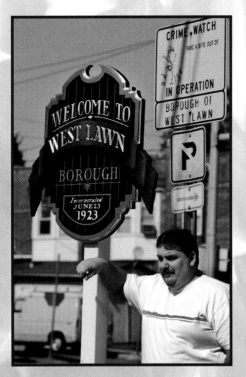

Different cities have different needs. In West Lawn, Pennsylvania, Mayor Richard A. Gould *(left)* believes there is no need for a city government in his town of 1,597 residents. "We conduct hardly any business at the council meetings other than paying bills," he said in 2002. Meanwhile, Mayor Jane Campbell *(right)* of Cleveland, Ohio, gets ready to give her State of the City speech in 2003. The speech is a general overview of the city given to the press and the public.

Mayors of larger cities work together to make their cities better. Mayors of cities with 30,000 or more people are members of the United States Conference of Mayors. The mayors in the conference meet to find ways to help their cities. They even meet with the president of the United States to help their cities.

Federal Aid

In 1932, mayors from across the country asked the federal government for help. The federal government runs the entire country. Millions of people were out of work and going hungry. The federal government gave a total of $300 million to cities around the country. This was the first time the federal government gave money to help cities.

The annual U.S. Conference of Mayors brings mayors from around the country together to discuss issues. President Bill Clinton is about to address the audience at the conference in 1997. Pictured *(left to right)* are Mayor Richard M. Daley of Chicago; Mayor Willie Brown of San Francisco; and Mayor Deedee Corradini of Salt Lake City.

The mayor's role is different in each city. Sometimes, the mayor shares power with the city council and other people in the government. Sometimes, the mayor has more power than anyone else in the government. Most cities have a city charter. The city charter tells what power each office will have.

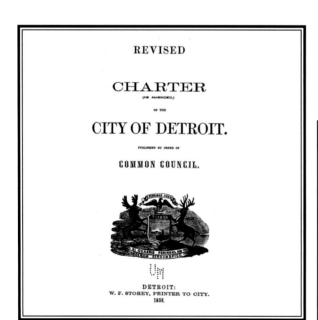

The city charter outlines the rules of government. The charter will explain the powers of each office. Pictured is a charter from Detroit, Michigan, from 1859.

The mayor has the power to assign people to certain important positions. Providence, Rhode Island, mayor David Cicilline *(left)* has just named Dean Esserman *(right)* the city's new police chief. Esserman's wife, Gilda, is pinning a police chief badge on her husband.

The mayor plays an important role in cities large or small. The choices a mayor makes help the city and the people who live there. You can help your mayor make your city a better place to live. How can your city be improved? Contact your mayor and let him or her know what you think!

Contacting your mayor is a great way to let him or her know about issues in the city. Here, Mayor Vera Katz of Portland, Oregon, speaks to a group of student protesters. The peaceful "sit-in" protest was held to rally against budget cuts in education.

Glossary

budget (BUH-jit)   A plan for how money will be earned and spent.
candidate (KAN-dih-dayt)   Someone who is applying for a job or running in an election.
city charter (SIH-tee CHAR-tur)   A formal document that states the rights or duties of a
   city government.
city council (SIH-tee KOWN-sul)   A group of people who help a mayor run a city.
conference (KON-fur-ens)   A group of people who meet to discuss ideas and opinions.
confiscated (KON-fih-skayt-ed)   Legally taken away.
department (dih-PART-ment)   A part of a city's government that has a particular function
   or purpose.
elected (ee-LEK-tid)   Having chosen someone or decided something by voting.
election (ee-LEK-shun)   The act or process of choosing someone or deciding something
   by voting.
federal (FEH-duh-rul)   Having to do with the central, or national, government.
mayor (MAY-er)   The leader of a town or city government.
taxes (TAKS-ez)   Money that people and businesses must pay in order to support
   a government.
term (TURM)   A definite or limited period of time.
vote (VOHT)   To make a choice in an election or other poll.

Web Sites

Due to the changing nature of Internet links, the Rosen Publishing Group, Inc., has developed
an online list of Web sites related to the subject of this book. This site is updated regularly.
Please use this link to access the list:

http://www.rosenlinks.com/pslac/yoma

Primary Source Image List

Cover (top right): New York City mayor Fiorello La Guardia photographed October 3, 1943.
Cover (bottom left): New York City mayor Michael Bloomberg photographed by Mario Tama,
June 9, 2002.
Cover (background): Letter by President George Washington to the Baltimore, Maryland, mayor and
city council, written in 1797 and archived by the Library of Congress.
Page 5 (top): Photo taken by John S. Stewart in Hermitage Hall, Missouri, April 16, 1996.
Page 5 (bottom): Photo of Richard M. Daley taken by David Zalubowski in Denver, Colorado,
May 18, 1996.

Page 7 (top): Photo by Nick Ut taken in Long Beach, California, June 4, 2002.
Page 7 (bottom): Photo of Sam Katz taken by Jacqueline Larma in Philadelphia, Pennsylvania, May 1, 2003.
Page 8: Photo by Jim Mone taken in Minneapolis, Minnesota, September 24, 1997.
Page 9: Photo by Daniel Hulshizer taken in Newark, New Jersey, May 14, 2002.
Page 10: Photo of San Francisco mayor Willie Brown taken by Randi Lynn Beach in San Francisco, November 2, 1999.
Page 11: Photo taken by Michael Dwyer in Providence, Rhode Island, November 5, 2002.
Page 13: Photo by Beth Keiser of New York City mayor Michael Bloomberg in New York City, February 13, 2002.
Page 14: Photo by Mike Derer taken in Newark, New Jersey, August 8, 2002.
Page 15: Photo taken by Cheryl Rower in Greenbrier, Alabama, on December 13, 2001.
Page 17: Photo of St. Louis mayor Francis Slay taken by James A. Finley, in St. Louis, Missouri, March 20, 2002.
Page 18: Photo by Silvan Morgan taken in Seattle, Washington, February 13, 2001.
Page 19: Photo of New York City mayor Fiorello La Guardia taken in New York City, October 3, 1934.
Page 20: Photo taken by Bill Moffitt in Hondo, New Mexico, on October 8, 2002.
Page 21: Photo of Salt Lake City mayor Deedee Corradini taken by Chery Gerber in New Orleans, Louisiana, June 11, 1999.
Page 22: Photo of Baltimore mayor Martin O'Malley in Baltimore, Maryland, February 14, 2003.
Page 23: Photo taken by Oscar Sosa in Jacksonville, Florida, on January 7, 2003.
Page 25 (left): Photo of West Lawn mayor Richard Gould, taken in West Lawn, Pennsylvania, May 1, 2002.
Page 25 (right): Cleveland mayor Jane Campbell photographed by Mark Duncan in Cleveland, Ohio, February 2, 2003.
Page 27: Photo by Wilfredo Lee, taken in San Francisco, California, on June 23, 1997.
Page 29: Photo by Victoria Arocho taken in Providence, Rhode Island, January 10, 2003.
Page 30: Photo of Portland mayor Vera Katz and protestors taken in Portland, Oregon, February 6, 2003.

Index

About the Author

Jennifer Silate is a freelance children's book author. She has written more than 100 books for children of all ages.